# The Young Scientist Investigates

# Materials

Terry Jennings

Oxford University Press

ISBN 0 19 918164 0 (Paperback)
ISBN 0 19 918170 5 (Hardback)

© Terry Jennings

First published 1984
Reprinted 1988, 1989, 1990, 1993

**Oxford University Press, Walton Street, Oxford OX2 6DP**

Oxford  New York  Toronto
Delhi  Bombay  Calcutta  Madras  Karachi
Kuala Lumpur  Singapore  Hong Kong  Tokyo
Nairobi  Dar es Salaam  Cape Town
Melbourne  Auckland  Madrid

and associated companies in
Berlin  Ibadan

*Oxford* is a trade mark of Oxford University Press

Phototypeset in Great Britain by
Tradespools Limited, Frome, Somerset
Printed in Hong Kong

## CONTENTS

# Materials we use

In our daily life we use thousands of things. All these things are made of materials. The buildings we live, work and play in are made of materials. So are our clothes. Furniture is made of materials, so are buses, trains, cars and ships.

Long ago, early people had very few materials. Some of their tools and weapons were made of stone and wood, or the antlers and horns of animals. Their clothes came from the fur and skins of animals.

Nowadays we use many different materials. Some of these materials are natural. They come from plants and animals. We use wool, leather, fur, silk and horn which come from animals. We use cotton, wood, rubber and linen which come from plants. Some natural materials such as stone, clay, gold, coal and oil are found in the ground.

We also use materials made by people. Iron, steel, glass, plastic and cement are all manufactured. But they are made from natural substances which we call raw materials.

1 wool    8 rubber    15 iron
2 leather   9 linen     16 steel
3 fur     10 stone   17 glass
4 silk    11 clay    18 plastic
5 horn   12 gold    19 cement
6 cotton 13 coal
7 wood  14 oil

# Wood

Wood is a natural material. It comes from trees. Some of our wood comes from trees with broad leaves, like oak, ash and beech. Nowadays much of our timber comes from forests planted by people. Most of these forests are of pine, fir and other conifers.

A conifer forest

Wood is used to make houses, furniture, boxes, fences and toys. It is also used to make telegraph poles, matchsticks, pencils, paper and cardboard. Wood can be easily cut, carved, shaped and polished. Some musical instruments are made of wood, and so are some boats and tool handles.

After a tree has been cut down its trunk is cut into thick planks. Before the wood can be used it has to be dried slowly and carefully. This is called seasoning. Sometimes the wood is dried in the open air. Sometimes it is dried in a special oven called a kiln. Warm air is blown between the planks.

Wood being seasoned

But not all wood is seasoned. As we shall see on page 6, a lot of wood is chopped up into small pieces and made into pulp. From this pulp, paper is made, and also artificial silk or rayon.

# Other ways of using wood

How veneer is made

Furniture being veneered

Sometimes logs of expensive kinds of wood are peeled into very thin sections. A thin layer of this expensive wood is stuck on to a cheaper wood. This thin layer of wood is called a veneer. Usually the veneer has an attractive pattern or grain on it. A lot of furniture is made from veneered wood.

Plywood

Plywood is made by sticking together thin sheets of wood. If you look at the edges of a piece of plywood, you can see how many layers of wood were used to make it.

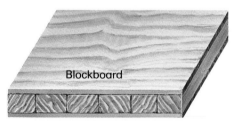

Blockboard

Blockboard is made from lengths of wood stuck together. These strips of wood are glued between two thin sheets of wood like a sandwich. Blockboard makes a very strong plank.

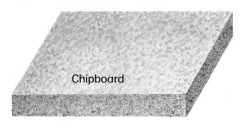

Chipboard

Chipboard is also a manufactured timber. Wood is chopped up into tiny pieces, or chips. These chips are mixed with glue and pressed into large boards. A lot of chipboard is used to make furniture, but first it is covered with a veneer.

# Paper

One common manufactured material is paper. Most paper is made from wood. The logs are first chopped up into small chips. The wood chips are then boiled with a chemical called caustic soda. This turns the wood chips into a soft, pulpy mass. The wood pulp looks a little like papier mâché. The pulp is bleached to make it white. The pulp is drained on a fine sieve and then it goes into the paper machine.

Wood chips for paper making

In the paper machine there is a large moving belt made of finely woven cloth. The pulp is spread over the belt as it moves along. A lot more of the water is gradually removed from the wood pulp. Then the pulp is pressed between large rollers which squeeze it out into a thin sheet. The paper is finished by passing it through heated rollers to make it smooth.

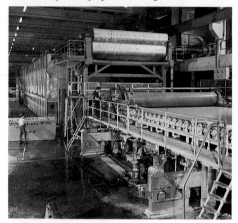
Paper-making machine

Paper is used for writing and printing. It is also used for wrapping and packing. Paper is used for tissues, tickets, bank notes and posters. It is even used for some kinds of clothing.

Paper coming from paper-making machine

# Rubber

Rubber is used for many things. A few of them are shown in the picture. Rubber is tough and it is waterproof. Rubber is elastic and it returns to its original shape when stretched or squashed. Most natural rubber comes from Malaysia.

Rubber is made from a white juice which comes from the rubber tree. This juice is called latex. To get the latex, a cut is made in the bark of a rubber tree. Under the cut a small cup is hung. Very, very slowly latex drips into the cup. The latex is collected and taken to a factory. Here acid is added to the latex. The acid makes the latex set to solid rubber. The rubber is rolled into flat sheets and dried ready to be sent overseas.

In the countries where rubber is used, the rubber sheets are sliced up by huge machines. The rubber becomes soft and sticky like chewing gum. A yellow substance called sulphur is added and the rubber is heated. This hardens the rubber so that it will bounce back into shape. The rubber can then be made into tyres and other things.

Even with millions of rubber trees we cannot make enough natural rubber for our needs. So synthetic or artificial rubber is made. It is made from chemicals which come from oil. For some things, synthetic rubber is better than natural rubber.

Collecting the latex from a rubber tree

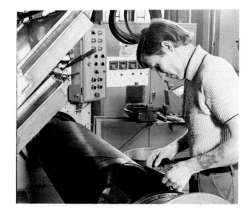

Car tyres being made

# Fibres

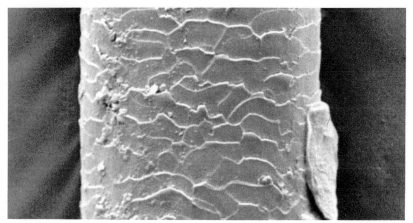

A fibre seen under a microscope

Picking cotton

Harvesting flax plants

Fibres are long thin threads of material. On their own, fibres are not very strong. But when some fibres are spun together they can be made into thread or rope. The thread can be woven into cloth.

Some fibres come from plants and some from animals. Nowadays many fibres are manufactured. Cotton fibres, from which thread and cloth are made, come from the seed pods of the cotton plant. Linen is made from fibres which come from the stem of the flax plant. Wood fibres are made into paper. Wool fibres, from which warm clothing is made, come from the hair of sheep.

A sheep being sheared

A silkworm

Silk comes from fibres made by silkworms. When a disease killed off many silkworms last century, scientists discovered how to make artificial silk. Today we call this 'artificial silk' rayon. Rayon is made from wood pulp. Rayon is mixed with wool or cotton to make clothes.

Another common fibre is nylon. As we shall see on page 10, nylon is made from oil or coal. Many kinds of clothes are made from nylon.

# Coal

One of the most useful materials is coal. People burn coal for fuel. They also make many chemicals from it. Dyes and paints are made from coal, so are explosives and aspirins. A few plastics, disinfectants and glues are made from coal. It is even possible to make oil and petrol from coal.

Millions of years ago, much of the land was covered by dense forest. The trees and other plants died and were covered by mud and sand. Very slowly the mud and sand were turned into rock. As more and more rock pressed down, the trees and other plants were slowly turned into coal. Huge machines are used to dig up the coal near the surface. The coal deeper down is dug up by miners working in tunnels.

In some countries, most of the coal used is burned in power stations to help make electricity. The ashes of the coal are used as a building material. Much coal is made into coke. Coal is heated in huge ovens to make coke. Gases come from the coal, and coke is left. Coke is cleaner than coal and it burns without a lot of smoke.

One of the many useful materials made when coal is heated to make coke is coal tar. Many chemicals can be made from coal tar and the gases which come from coal when it is heated.

Some of the things we make from coal

Coal-cutting machine

Hot coke coming from the ovens

9

# Oil

Oil is another important material. It is used as a fuel. We use oil to heat our houses, shops and factories. Oil is used to drive trains, buses, lorries and ships. Oil is also used as a lubricant to stop the parts of machines rubbing together and wearing out. Oil can be made into many other materials. Some of the many things made from oil are petrol, plastics, jet fuel, nylon, floor polish and records. Even the ink with which newspapers are printed is made from oil. Bitumen, the black tarry substance put on roads and aircraft runways, is made from oil.

Oil was formed from the bodies of tiny sea plants and animals which lived long ago. Layers of rock later pressed down on these tiny plants and animals and turned them into oil. To reach the oil, deep holes have to be drilled into the ground. Sometimes the drilling takes place under the sea. A large floating drilling rig is used to drill for the oil if the sea is deep. The holes are lined with pipes as they are drilled. Big pipes or ships carry the oil ashore.

Man oiling a machine

A floating oil-drilling rig

# Do you remember?

(Look for the answers in the part of the book you have just been reading if you do not know them.)

1 Name four natural materials.

2 Name four manufactured materials.

3 What are raw materials?

4 What kind of tree does most of our wood come from?

5 What happens to wood when it is being seasoned?

6 What is made from wood pulp?

7 How is wood pulp made?

8 What is latex?

9 What is synthetic or artificial rubber made from?

10 Why is rubber a useful material?

11 What do fibres look like?

12 Where do fibres come from?

13 Where does silk come from?

14 Where do cotton and linen fibres come from?

15 How was coal formed?

16 How is coal obtained from the ground?

17 Name five materials which can be made from coal.

18 From what was oil formed?

19 How did the rocks help produce oil?

20 Give five uses of oil.

# Things to do

**1 Sorting materials into groups.**
Scientists spend a lot of their time sorting things into groups. They call this classifying. Classify some common materials you can find in your home or classroom into three groups.

In one group put things which are transparent or clear, like a glass milk bottle or a drinking tumbler.

In another group put things you cannot see through at all, such as a nail or a knife. These things are called opaque.

In the third group put things which are translucent. These are things that let light through them but which you cannot see through, such as some lampshades and coloured glass bottles.

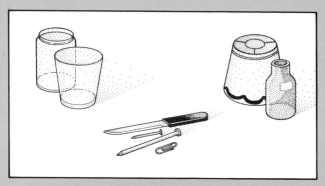

Find other ways of classifying materials, such as those which feel heavy for their size and thickness, and those which feel light for their size and thickness. Have a third group which comes in between these other groups.

Another way of classifying materials is to see which of them make static electricity. If you rub a comb or pen on a piece of woollen cloth or on the sleeve of a coat, it will attract tiny pieces of tissue paper when it is held over them. Which other materials pick up tiny pieces of tissue paper when rubbed in this way? Which materials do not make static electricity?

**2   A time-machine.** Pretend you have a time-machine which will allow you to go back into the past. Pretend that you go back thousands of years to the time when the only materials available were the skins or furs of animals, flints and other stones, and wood and the parts of trees and other plants. Write a story about a day in your life. What is the countryside around you like? What wild animals are there? What do you eat? How do you collect or catch your food? How do you protect yourself from wild animals and other dangers and keep yourself warm?

**3   Leather, fur and animal skins.** Name some animals which give us leather. From which kinds of animals do we get fur or skins? What sort of things do we make from leather, fur, and animal skins? What kinds of materials made by people could we use instead of leather, fur and animal skins? Would these materials be better or worse? Why?

**4   Knots in wood.** The side branches in a tree make small rings and ovals in the wood when it is cut into planks. Often the knots have beautiful waves around them, and wood with knots in it is used in some fine furniture. Draw some knots in wood carefully and colour them. Sometimes plastic is printed to imitate the pattern of knots on wood and is used as a veneer on furniture.

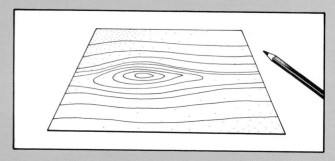

**5   Collect samples of paper.** Collect pieces of as many different kinds of paper as you can find. From each kind of paper cut three pieces all the same size. For each kind of paper use one small piece to see how easy it is to write on. Use another piece to see how good it is at soaking up water. Use the third piece to see how easily it tears. For each kind of paper, say whether it is rough, smooth on both sides, or smooth on one side only.

**6 A map of treasure island.** Have you ever seen pictures in story books of maps showing where buried treasure is to be found? Make your own map of treasure island on white paper. Give clues as to where to find the treasure. Tear around the outside of the map to make it look frayed and old. Usually old maps are a faded brown colour. You can make your map look very old by dipping it into cold tea and then leaving it to dry.

**7 Papier mâché.** Make some papier mâché. Tear up old newspapers or tissues into small pieces – the smaller the pieces the better. Get a bowl of water and add a little wallpaper paste to the water and stir it in. If you do not have any wallpaper paste, you can use flour-and-water paste. Soak the pieces of paper in the liquid, stirring it from time to time.

When you get a good pulpy mass, squeeze the liquid out of it. Mould the papier mâché into the shape you want. The heads of people (or puppets) and animals, and simple shapes like owls, are easy to make. Leave the shape to dry in a warm room. In a few days it will dry hard, like the wood the fibres originally came from. Paint your shapes.

**8 Make your own paper.** As we saw on page 6, paper is made from wood fibres. It is not easy to get the fibres from wood without the use of dangerous chemicals, but you can make paper from the fibres of soft-tissue toilet-rolls. If possible use different coloured toilet tissues as this makes the fibres easier to see.

Put about a litre of water in a bowl and add about 12 sheets of toilet tissue to it. Stir the tissues thoroughly until they break up and are spread throughout the water.

Dip a piece of fine wire gauze about 15 centimetres × 10 centimetres, into the fibres. If you cannot get fine wire gauze you could nail a piece of fine muslin (or a piece of a pair of tights) on to a wooden frame about 15 centimetres × 10 centimetres.

Lift out the wire gauze or the wooden frame and shake it gently so that the fibres settle and the water drains away.

Turn the wire or frame over and press the sheet of fibres on to a piece of felt. Cover the sheet of fibres with a second piece of felt and roll it firmly with a rolling pin or a large bottle.

Remove the top felt. If the paper you have made sticks, take it off gently and put it back on the bottom felt. Now lay a third piece of felt on top of the paper. Leave the paper in a warm room to dry.

Try making new paper from old newspapers, blotting paper, thin card or paper towelling.

**9  Rubber trees.** Brazil, Malaysia, Indonesia and Sri Lanka are countries which grow a lot of rubber trees. Look at a map of the world and find these places. What line on the map goes through or near these countries? What does it tell you about the climate of these countries?

**10  Woollen and cotton clothing.** What items of clothing are often made out of wool? Which are made of cotton? If you were outside on a hot, sunny day would you wear woollen clothes or cotton clothes? Why? Which clothes would you wear on a cold, frosty day?

**11  Natural and artificial fibres.** Many clothes are made from a mixture of natural and artificial fibres. Look at the labels in the clothes you are wearing. Write down the names of all the fibres mentioned on the labels. Try to find out which fibres are artificial and which are natural.

**12  Weaving.** Weave some cloth of your own. Cut a square of stiff card and cut notches on two sides as shown in the picture.

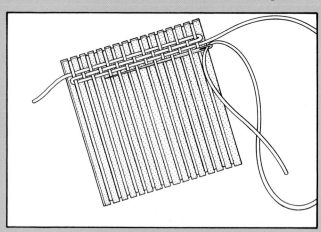

For your first attempts at weaving, use thin string or wool. Fix the thread at one corner with a small piece of Sellotape. Wind a length of thread around the card. Keep the thread tight and even.

Now use a large darning needle to weave a piece of thread of a different colour. Do not weave too close to the notches in the card.

Carefully cut the loops of thread around the cardboard notches so that the cloth comes away.

Now try weaving with finer threads of different colours. What kinds of patterns can you make?

**13  Fluffy woollen balls and toys.** Take a piece of cardboard. A piece from a box will do. Draw a circle on it about 6 centimetres in diameter. Draw another circle 2 centimetres in diameter around the centre of the first one. Cut around the big circle. Cut out the small circle as shown in the picture.

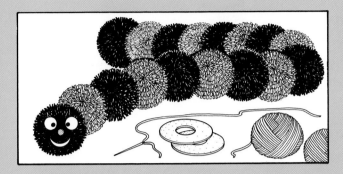

Now do the same thing again, so that you finish up with two rings of cardboard, both exactly the same size.

Take a small ball of 3 or 4 ply wool. Start with a piece of the wool about 2 metres long. Tie the end of the wool through the hole in the middle of both pieces of cardboard. Wind the wool evenly round and round the two rings of cardboard. Do not pull the wool too tight. If needs be, tie more wool on to the end of the length of wool you started with. Use a large sewing needle to thread the wool through the hole as it gets smaller and smaller. Do this until you cannot get any more wool on the cardboard and tie a knot. Cut across the cardboard without cutting the wool (*careful!*), and pull away the cardboard. Fluff out the finished ball.

Make other larger or smaller fluffy balls. Join some together to make a caterpillar like the one in the picture. Give the caterpillar eyes and a mouth cut from thin felt.

**14 Fibres and fabrics.** Take a small piece of coarse fabric. Sacking or hessian is ideal. Look at it with a hand lens or magnifying glass. Draw a picture to show how the fabric was woven. Take the piece

of fabric apart and see how it is made. The thread or yarn is made of fibres twisted together. Can you see the separate fibres in a thread or yarn?

Use Sellotape to stick a small piece of the fabric, a thread or yarn and a fibre on to a sheet of paper. Next to them put the drawing you made. Label these with the name of the fabric they came from.

Now study other fabrics in this way.

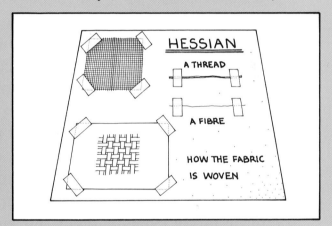

**15 Compare different fabrics.** Hold a piece of fabric up to the light. Are there spaces between the threads or yarns?

Cut a strip of fabric 1 centimetre wide. Take out the threads or yarns. How many are there in the piece of fabric 1 centimetre wide?

Take out a thread or yarn 10 centimetres long. Look at it with a hand lens or magnifying glass. Is it bristly? Why? Untwist the thread to see how long the fibres are. Do they run the whole length of the thread?

Now look at other fabrics in this way and write notes on what you discover.

# Iron and steel

Most of the metals we use are found in rocks. Rocks with lots of metal in them are called ores. Iron is found in rocks. One kind of iron ore is shown in the picture.

Iron ore

The ore must be heated in a big fire or furnace to get the metal out. To make iron, the ore is heated with coke and limestone in a big furnace.

Iron is used nowadays mainly for making steel. This is done by blowing oxygen through the molten iron in a special furnace, called a converter. Steel is stronger than iron and can be flattened, shaped or pulled out into wire. This cannot be done with iron, which is brittle. Steel can also be made in electric furnaces, using steel scrap instead of iron. By adding other substances while it is still molten, the steel can be made even stronger. Or substances can be added to prevent it from rusting. This is called making stainless steel. Some of the many things made from steel are pictured below

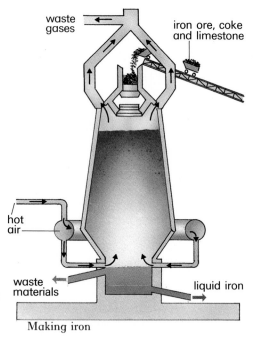

Making iron

A steel-making converter

16

# Some other metals

A piece of copper ore and copperware

Aluminium is being used to make this railway coach

A piece of gold

Copper is an important metal. Copper is made from copper ore. There is a piece of copper ore in the picture. Copper metal itself is a reddish colour. Electricity passes along copper well and so copper is used for making wires and cables. Heat passes quickly through copper, and so it is used for boilers and some saucepans. Copper pipes do not rust or rot, and they can easily be bent. Copper pipes are used to carry hot and cold water in buildings. Modern coins also contain a lot of copper.

Aluminium is a very light metal. It is made from aluminium ore which is found in the ground. Because it is light, a lot of aluminium is used to make aircraft and the bodies of buses and railway coaches and containers. Because it lets heat pass through it and does not rust, a lot of aluminium is used in pots and pans. Aluminium is also used for milk bottle tops and some drink cans and, when very thin, to cover chocolate bars.

Unlike iron, copper and aluminium, gold is found as the pure metal. Tiny pieces of gold are sometimes washed out of rocks into the gravel in the bottom of streams and rivers. Treasure hunters search the gravel for gold. Gold is mined in many countries including South Africa, Australia, Russia, North and South America and Wales. Gold is used for jewellery, ornaments, some coins, and to repair teeth.

# Sand, gravel and clay

Sand, gravel and clay are natural materials. They all come from rocks which have been broken down by the weather. The sun, rain, wind and frost broke the rock down into small pieces. Often, the pieces of rock were washed away by streams and rivers into the sea. As the pieces of rock were carried along by the water, they were broken into smaller and smaller pieces. In some places, thousands of years ago, the pieces of rock were carried along by rivers of ice called glaciers.

Gravel consists of pieces of rock that are larger than those which make up sand. The pieces of rock in gravel have been worn smooth by rivers and the sea. Gravel is used to make concrete. Sand consists of tiny grains of rock. We can play with sand and mould it. Concrete and glass are made from sand. Sand glued to paper (sandpaper) is used to smooth wood.

Clay is made up of the tiniest pieces of rock. The pieces are so tiny that they stick together like plasticine. Clay can be fired in a large oven, or kiln, to make bricks and tiles. The finest kinds of clay can be made into china and other kinds of pottery. Clay can be heated in a kiln, with limestone, to make cement. Sand, gravel and clay are dug out of the ground from large pits. All buildings and roads are made with the help of sand, gravel and clay.

Rocks which have been broken down by the weather

A sand and gravel pit

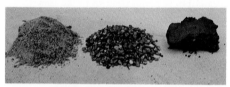
Sand gravel and clay

Making a clay pot on a wheel

# Cement and concrete

Bags of cement powder

Cement is made here.

Unloading concrete from a mixer lorry

Cement is a very important building material. It is a grey powder. Cement is made from chalk or limestone and clay. The chalk or limestone and the clay are all rocks. They are dug out of the ground. To make cement, the chalk or limestone and clay are put in a large oven called a kiln. In the very hot kiln, the chalk or limestone and the clay are roasted. When the roasted lumps are cooled they are crushed into a powder. This is cement.

The builder uses the cement powder to make mortar and concrete. To make mortar, cement is mixed with sand and water. Mortar is used to join bricks or concrete blocks together when a wall is being built.

To make concrete, sand and gravel are mixed with cement and water. Sometimes the concrete is mixed by hand. More often a concrete mixer is used. If very large quantities are needed, the concrete may be mixed at the factory. Then the wet concrete is delivered to the building site in a mixer lorry like the one in the picture. Concrete is used to make roads, buildings, paths, bridges and the foundations of houses. Often the concrete is reinforced or strengthened with pieces of steel.

# Glass

Glass was invented by the Egyptians. It was first made about 5000 years ago. Glass is made by heating together sand, washing soda and limestone. These substances are heated in a furnace. The furnace is very hot and the sand, washing soda and limestone melt and join together to form glass. The melted glass is poured into moulds to make shapes. Sometimes a blob of molten glass is put on the end of a long metal tube. Air is blown down the tube into the molten glass. The tube is turned and the molten glass is blown into beautiful shapes.

Glass is used for ornaments, jars, bottles and windows. Glass is also used for building and for making cooking bowls and dishes. Very pure glass is used to make lenses. Binoculars, telescopes, cameras, spectacles and microscopes are just a few of the things which have lenses in them.

Molten glass can be pulled out into thin threads. This is called glass fibre. Glass fibre is used to make some boats, cars, fishing rods and curtains. It can also be used to make the insulation put in roofs to keep houses warm.

Glass blowing

A stained glass window

# Plastics

Nowadays we use more and more plastics. Plastics are used instead of materials like wood, metal and glass. Plastics are cheap and easier to make. They are light, they do not rust or rot, and many of them are difficult to break.

Electric plugs and switches made from plastic

Plastics are made from chemicals which come from oil. There are many kinds of plastics. Heat does not pass easily through plastics, so they can be used for the handles of saucepans and kettles. Electricity does not pass through plastics. This means plastics can be used to cover wires, switches and plugs which carry electricity.

A plastic toy being moulded

Plastics can be coloured and moulded into any shape. Buckets, bowls, bottles, toys, pens, combs and many other things can be shaped from plastics. Some plastics are bendy, some are rigid. Some are tough, some break easily. Some are transparent, others are opaque. Some plastics can be drawn out into fine fibres. Others can be made into flat sheets. Nowadays plastics have thousands of uses in our homes, schools, factories, shops, gardens and farms.

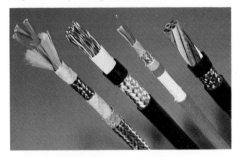
Plastic-covered electricity cables

# Different kinds of plastics

Plastics have names which are often difficult to
remember. Here are five common kinds of plastic:
nylon, polythene and polypropylene, PVC,
(Poly Vinyl Chloride), polystyrene, and perspex
or acrylic.
The pictures show some of the many things
made from each of the five common kinds of plastic.

Nylon

PVC

Polystyrene

Polythene and polypropylene

Acrylic or perspex

# New things from old

We throw away lots of things when we have finished with them. Many of the things we throw away are of no use. But the materials of which they are made could be used again. We throw away lots of waste paper. We throw away lots of glass jars and bottles. We dump old cars, machinery and metal containers. Many people think we can waste materials for ever, but we cannot.

Not only is dumped rubbish nasty to look at, it is very wasteful. If we go on using up some materials at the present rate, soon there will be none left. The best way to get rid of waste materials is to find a use for them. In some towns the rubbish is burnt and the heat is used to make electricity or to warm buildings. Waste paper and rags can be used to make new paper and cardboard. That way we have to cut down fewer trees. Some kinds of plastics can be melted down and made into new ones.

Some buildings in Nottingham are heated by rubbish brought here and burnt.

Using materials again in this way is called recycling. The more we recycle materials instead of wasting them, the longer we can make the natural materials last.

# Do you remember?

(Look for the answers in the part of the book you have just been reading if you do not know them.)

1  What do we call rocks which have a lot of metal in them?

2  Name the three things which are heated together to make iron.

3  Why is steel better than iron for some things?

4  How is steel made?

5  Why is copper used to make the water pipes used in buildings?

6  Why is copper used to make electrical wires and cables?

7  Name four things which are made from aluminium.

8  What does aluminium look like?

9  How is gold obtained from rocks?

10  How were sand, gravel and clay formed?

11  What is gravel used for?

12  What are three uses of sand?

13  What is clay used for?

14  What does cement look like?

15  How is cement made?

16  How is concrete made?

17  What substances are used to make glass?

18  Name five things which are made from glass.

19  Why are plastics often used instead of materials like wood, metal and glass?

20  Why are plastics used to cover the wires, plugs and switches which carry electricity?

21  Name three kinds of plastics.

22  What could be made from waste paper and rags?

23  What do we call it when we use waste materials again?

# Things to do

1  **Shiny metals.** Collect samples of different kinds of metals. Clean these samples with emery paper and then polish them with metal polish. Does the colour of the metal change? Write down what each metal looked like before it had been cleaned and what it looked like after.

Many metals go dull when they are left in the air, especially if the air is damp. We say the metals tarnish. Put some samples of metal you have polished on a piece of wood outside. Look at them every day for a month or so. What happens to each of the metals?

Whereabouts in the home, garage, school or road can you see metals which are shiny and which do not tarnish easily? Try to find out what these metals are called.

**2 Gold.** Collect pictures of jewellery and other things which are made of gold. Make a book or wallchart with your pictures. Write a sentence or two about each one.

**3 Stained glass windows.** Look at the stained glass windows in churches and other old buildings. Look carefully at how the picture in the window is made up of small pieces of coloured glass which fit together like the pieces of a jigsaw puzzle. Draw part of a stained glass window and colour it.

You could make your own stained glass window using pieces of coloured tissue paper. With permission, stick the pieces on to the glass of a real window. Surround the picture you have made with a frame made from black paper.

**4 Safety glass.** Ordinary glass, like that used in bottles and house windows, can break into very sharp pieces. Car windows and the glass doors in schools are often made of special safety glass. Look carefully at the glass in car windows and school doors. How is it different from ordinary window glass? Find out all you can about this safety glass and how it behaves if it is broken.

**5 Heat conductors and insulators.** Some materials allow heat to pass through them very easily. Aluminium allows heat to pass through it easily. That is why saucepans and kettles are often made of this metal. Aluminium feels cold to the touch. That is because it carries heat away from your fingers easily. Aluminium and other materials which feel cold to the touch are *conductors* of heat.

Some other materials feel warm to the touch. Wood and plastic, for example, feel warm. Wood and plastic do not carry heat away from your fingers quickly. They are said to be heat *insulators*.

Make lists of materials that feel cold to the touch (conductors) and those which feel warm (insulators). Say what each of these materials is used for.

**6  Old pits.** Sand, gravel, clay, limestone, chalk, iron ore and sometimes even coal, come from large holes or pits dug in the ground. What happens to these pits when all the material has been taken from them? From a *safe distance*, make drawings or take photographs of old pits in your area. Make a wallchart or book of your pictures. Write a sentence or two about each one saying what was obtained from the pit, when work there stopped, and what has happened to the pit since then.

**7  Waste paper.** As we saw on page 6, paper is made from trees. But the world's trees are being cut down very rapidly to make paper and to make way for houses, factories, roads and farms. Paper can also be made from waste paper. For every 1 tonne of waste paper used again in this way, 17 trees are saved.

Ask your teacher if you can organise a waste paper collection in your school. The paper could be sold to raise money for a charity or for your school funds. Not only will you be helping to raise money for a good cause you will also be saving precious trees.

**8  Junk models.** As we saw on page 23, recycling materials is finding a new use for them rather than throwing them away. If we make junk models we are really recycling waste. How many different models and useful things can you make from plastic washing-up liquid bottles? Some examples are shown in the picture to give you some ideas. Paint your models when you have finished making them.

Make a display of your models in your classroom.

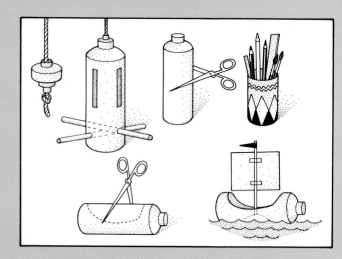

**9  Collecting materials for charity.** Several charities ask people to collect used postage stamps, tin foil, aluminium foil or the metal tabs from drinks cans. These materials are sold to raise money to buy guide dogs for the blind, medicines for the ill, and food for the hungry. Find out the address of one of these charities. Organise a collection of materials in your school or amongst your friends. How can you use a magnet to decide which cans are made of aluminium and which are made of steel?

**10  Litter.** How much waste material do we throw away in our dustbins in a week? Ask your parents if the rubbish can be put into separate bags – paper in one, tin cans and other metal objects in another, glass in another, and all other kinds of rubbish in a fourth. At the end of the week, weigh each bag to see how much waste material it contains. You might also be able to find out how much waste comes from your school in a day, using the same method.

|  | Glass | Drinks cans | Cigarette packets | Sweet papers | Crisp bags | Ice cream wrappers | Lollipop sticks | Orange peel and apple cores |
|---|---|---|---|---|---|---|---|---|
| Green Road | | | | | | | | |
| Swift Road | | | | | | | | |
| Playing field | | | | | | | | |
| Beach | | | | | | | | |

**11 A litter survey.** Carry out a litter survey near your home or school. Draw a table like this one, writing in the names of some of the roads or other places near your home or school.

Record the number of items of each kind of litter that you find in each place. Only do this survey somewhere safe and with the permission of your parents or a teacher. Avoid busy streets and stay on the pavement.

Where is the nearest litter bin? Is it full? What is the most common kind of litter in each of the places you looked at?

Can you find out who drops most litter: men, women, boys or girls?

**12 Design a poster.** Design a poster to discourage people from leaving litter. Keep the design simple and put a message on the poster which will make people think before they drop litter.

**13 Recycling materials.** Why will recycling materials like glass and iron and steel lead not only to a tidier countryside, but also to fewer big holes in the ground?

**14 Supplies of materials.** The graph below shows when scientists believe the supplies of some important materials will be used up, if we go on using them at the present rate.

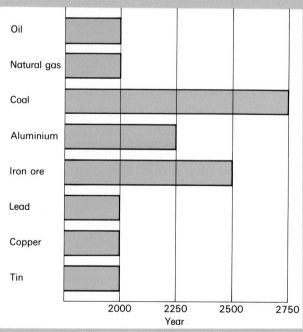

Calculate how much longer we have got to use each of these materials.

What are these materials used for? What can we use instead of these materials when there is none left? Will life be easier or more difficult than it is now?

# Experiments to try

Do your experiments carefully. Write or draw what you have done and what happens. Say what you have learned. Compare your findings with those of your friends.

## 1  Sorting Materials

On page 11, we saw one way of sorting or classifying materials. In this experiment we are going to look at some more ways of sorting or classifying materials.

*What you need:* A collection of small pieces of materials of different kinds (for a fair experiment, ideally the pieces should all be the same size); a bowl of water; a magnet; a battery; a lampholder and bulb; three pieces of wire; two drawing pins and a small block of wood; a large nail.

*What you do:* Look at each of the materials in turn. Write down what colour each one is and whether it is smooth or rough, dull or shiny. Use the large nail to see whether each material is easy or difficult to scratch.

Next see whether each material floats or sinks when it is placed in a bowl of water.

Test each material to see whether or not it is picked up by a magnet.

Finally connect up the battery, the lampholder and bulb, the wires, and the block of wood and drawing pins as shown in the picture. Lay the nail across the two drawing pins and the bulb should light. If it does not, then check that all the connections are tight. Now lay each of your materials in turn across the drawing pins. Does the bulb light? A material which electricity flows through so that the bulb lights up is called a *conductor* of electricity. A material which does not allow electricity to pass, so that the bulb does not light up, is called an *insulator*.

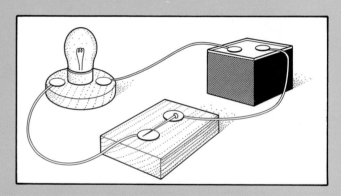

Make a table of your discoveries like this:

| Material | Colour and texture | Is it easy or difficult to scratch ? | Does it sink or float in water ? | Can it be picked up by a magnet ? | Does the bulb light ? | Conductor or insulator of electricity ? |
|---|---|---|---|---|---|---|
| Piece of glass | Transparent and shiny | Difficult | Sinks | No | No | Insulator |
| Iron nail | Grey and shiny | Difficult | Sinks | Yes | Yes | Conductor |

## 2 Which is the hardest-wearing fabric?

*What you need:* A brick; pieces of fabric of different kinds – all the same size (strips about 15 centimetres wide and 30 to 35 centimetres long are easiest to handle); a thick newspaper.

*What you do:* Lay the brick on a thick newspaper on a desk or table.

Take one of the pieces of fabric. Hold one end of the fabric in each hand and rub the fabric backwards and forwards across the brick.

Count how many rubs it takes until a small hole appears in the fabric. The hole has been made because little pieces of the fibres in the fabric are broken off by rough bits that stick out from the brick.

Now do the same thing with other pieces of fabric.

For your tests to be fair, you must use pieces of fabric which are all the same size and use equally hard rubs. The brick must be the same one in all parts of the experiment.

Which kind of fabric is the most hardwearing? In what kinds of clothing would it be important to have hardwearing fabrics?

Are cotton sheets harder-wearing than nylon sheets? Are jeans harder-wearing than nylon, woollen or other kinds of trousers?

## 3 Bouncing things

It is not only rubber balls which bounce, as we shall see in this experiment.

*What you need:* A desk or table; a piece of card; sticky tape; tennis ball; solid rubber ball; ping-pong ball; pen or pencil; set of scales.

You will also need a friend to help you.

*What you do:* Tape a strip of card to the leg of a desk or table. Carefully drop the tennis ball from the top of the table or desk above the leg which has the card taped to it. Ask your friend to use a pen or pencil to mark on the card how high the tennis ball bounces. Weigh the tennis ball.

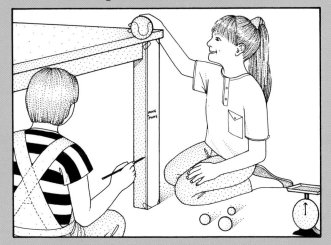

Now measure how high each of the other balls bounces. Weigh each ball.

Is it the biggest or the heaviest ball which bounces the highest? What is the best bouncer made of? Is it solid or hollow in the centre?

If you repeat this experiment using a higher desk, table or shelf, does the ball bounce higher? Why is this?

## 4  Testing the strength of concrete

Concrete is made by mixing together gravel, sand and cement with water. The gravel, sand and cement have to be in the right proportions, though.

*What you need:* Cement, sand and gravel; plastic margarine tubs for measuring; old spoons or trowels for stirring and mixing; two pieces of wood about 20 centimetres long and 4 or 5 centimetres wide and deep; two other pieces of wood about 45 centimetres long and 4 or 5 centimetres wide and deep; some strong rubber bands; a plank of wood; some old newspapers; some weights; a plastic bucket.

*What you do:* Mixing concrete is messy and is best done outside.

Arrange the strips of wood as shown in the picture and hold them in place with strong rubber bands. Make the space inside this mould 30 centimetres long. Lay the mould on several sheets of newspaper on top of the plank.

Mix up the cement, sand and gravel. Measure these out using the margarine tubs. Start with a mixture of 1 part of cement to 2 parts of sand and 4 parts of gravel. Mix these together thoroughly and then add a little water and mix again. Add only enough water to make a really stiff mixture. Do not make the mixture too wet.

Carefully put the mixture in the mould and smooth off the top. If you find you have not made enough concrete, quickly mix up some more with the same proportions of cement, sand and gravel and add it to the first lot.

Leave the concrete for several days to set hard and then take away the wooden mould.

Now make some more concrete bars exactly the same size as the first. Make them with different proportions of sand, gravel and cement, though. Label the finished bars so that you know which is which.

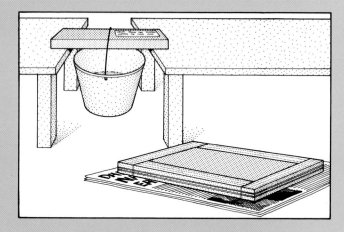

Test the strength of one of your concrete bars by hanging a plastic bucket from it as shown in the picture. Make sure the bucket is exactly in the middle of the bar. Also make sure that the same length of bar is resting on the tables or supports at each end. Have the bucket as near to the floor as possible to avoid damage or injury.

Now carefully put weights in the bucket, one at a time. Instead of weights you could measure out cups or margarine tubs of sand. Keep adding weights until the bar breaks (mind your feet!). Record how many weights it took to break the bar.

Go on now to find out how strong the other bars are. Does more cement make the bars stronger?

What happens if you compare other concrete bars made with the same proportions of cement, sand and gravel, but adding more water to one than the other? What happens if the sand or gravel is left out?

Try reinforcing one bar with a metal knitting needle while the concrete mixture is being put into the mould. Compare the strength of this bar with that of another bar made in the same way but without reinforcing.

## 5 What happens to waste paper and other litter?

Some people are careless or thoughtless and leave a lot of untidy litter around. What happens if no-one picks it up?

*What you need:* Some waste wrapping materials. You could include a sweet wrapper, a piece of newspaper, writing paper, a paper tissue, a piece of cardboard and a plastic bag; an apple core; some orange peel; a tin can and a plastic bottle; some stones or wooden pegs.

*What you do:* Cut the pieces of wrapping materials so that they are all the same size. Fix them to the soil in a garden or flower bed with stones or wooden pegs. Carefully draw a plan of the position of each of the materials, so that you can find them and identify them later. Peg down the apple core and piece of orange peel as well, and lay the tin can and plastic bottle on the soil.

After a month look carefully at each of the materials. How have they changed?

Leave them for another month and then look at the materials again. Which kinds of litter take the longest to rot away?

## 6 Which materials does heat go through?

*What you need:* A rubber hot-water bottle, a piece of wood, a plastic plate, a china plate, a flat piece of metal, some cardboard and paper, pieces of woollen and cotton materials.

*What you do:* Ask your teacher to fill the hot-water bottle with hot water for you. Lay the hot-water bottle on the table. Quickly touch the outside of the bottle. Is it hot?

Now lay the piece of wood on top of the bottle. Leave it there for a few minutes. Put your hand on top of the piece of wood. Does it feel hot? Does it feel warm?

Next lay the piece of metal on top of the hot-water bottle. Leave it for a few minutes. Now put your hand on the metal. Is it hotter or colder than the wood was?

Now try the experiment with other materials. Make lists of those materials which let the heat through quickly and those which let the heat through slowly. Materials which let heat through quickly are called heat conductors. Those which let heat through slowly are called heat insulators. Which of the materials you used are heat conductors and which are heat insulators?

# Glossary

Here are the meanings of some words which you might have met for the first time in this book.

**Bitumen:** the black, tarry substance used to make roads.

**Coke:** a fuel which is made by heating coal in huge ovens. Coke is cleaner than coal and burns without smoke.

**Conductors:** materials through which heat or electricity can pass easily.

**Conifers:** trees which do not have proper flowers although they do have separate male and female parts. The female parts develop into cones which contain seeds. Most conifers have needle-shaped leaves like those of pine and spruce trees.

**Disinfectants:** chemicals used to kill germs in rooms and on clothes.

**Fibres:** long thin hair-like strands of material.

**Fuel:** anything that will burn.

**Glacier:** a river of ice.

**Insulators:** materials through which heat or electricity cannot pass easily.

**Kiln:** a large oven in which materials like bricks, pottery, metals and cement are made.

**Latex:** the juice or sap of the rubber tree. From latex rubber is made.

**Linen:** a kind of cloth made from fibres which come from the stem of the flax plant.

**Lubricant:** a substance such as oil which is used to stop the parts of machines rubbing together and wearing out.

**Materials:** the substances from which things are made.

**Mortar:** cement mixed with sand and water. Mortar is used to join bricks together when making a wall.

**Nylon:** a material made from fibres which are made from coal or oil.

**Ores:** rocks with a lot of metal in them.

**Plastics:** a group of substances which can be shaped or moulded into any form. Plastics are made from chemicals which come from oil.

**Rayon:** artificial silk.

**Recycling:** using materials again instead of wasting them.

**Seasoning:** the slow, careful drying of wood before it can be used to make things.

**Silk:** a kind of cloth made from fibres made by silkworms.

**Synthetic rubber:** artificial rubber which is made from chemicals which come from oil.

**Veneer:** a thin layer of expensive wood which is stuck on to cheaper wood.

The publishers would like to thank the following for permission to reproduce transparencies:

Avon Rubber plc: p. 7 (bottom); B.P. Oil Ltd: p. 10 (bottom right); British Rail Engineering Ltd: p. 17 (centre); British Railways Board: p. 10 (centre); British Steel Corporation: p. 16 (top); J. Allan Cash Ltd: p. 16 (bottom right), p. 23 (centre); Cement and Concrete Association: p. 19 (top, 2nd from top, 2nd from bottom, bottom); L.C. Marigo/Bruce Coleman: p. 8 (top right), Jane Burton/Bruce Coleman: p. 8 (bottom); Fothergill and Harvey plc: p. 17 (2nd from top), p. 21 (2nd from bottom); Habitat Designs Ltd: p. 21 (top); Sam Herman: p. 20 (top, centre); Hilly Janes: p. 4 (bottom), p. 7 (2nd from bottom), p. 8 (2nd from bottom); Terry Jennings: p. 4 (top), p. 10 (top), p. 17 (2nd from bottom), p. 18 (top, 2nd from top, 2nd from bottom), p. 23 (top); Lambeg Industrial Research Association: p. 8 (2nd from top); Lego System A/S: p. 21 (2nd from top); Malaysian Rubber Producers' Research Association: p. 7 (2nd from top); Mark Mason: p. 4 (centre), p. 6 (bottom), p. 7 (top), p. 9 (top), p. 16 (bottom left), p. 20 (bottom left), p. 21 (bottom); National Coal Board: p. 9 (centre, bottom); Nottingham City Council: p. 23 (bottom left); Joseph Nutgens: p. 20 (bottom right); David Kerr/Oxford Scientific Films: p. 8 (top left); Rosemarie Pitts: p. 18 (bottom); PPP Industrial Training Board: p. 23 (bottom right); Shell Photo Service: p. 10 (bottom left); St. Regis Paper Co (UK) Ltd, Silverton Mill: p. 6 (2nd from bottom); Timber Research and Development Association: p. 5 (top); Titchmarsh and Goodwin: p. 5 (centre); The Wiggins Teape Group Ltd: p. 6 (top, 2nd from bottom).

The publishers would like to thank the following for loaning items to be photographed:-

Benfields Garage, Deddington; John Farmer Ltd; Gill and Co (Ironmongers) Ltd; Oxford and Swindon Co-operative Society Ltd; Jonathan Patterson (Pine Furniture); Rollers (Oxford); Science Studio (Oxford) Ltd; Scoops (Woodstock); Stockland (Oxford).

Illustrated by Karen Daws    Tony Morris    Coral Mula    Tudor Artists